THE
MIRROR
HOLDS THE
FLAME

Ahmed
Mustafa

Hidayah
Publishers

The Mirror Holds the Flame

ISBN (Paperback): 978-1-998843-52-7

Printed in the United States of America

CONTENTS

Preface

There's a quiet hope we all share–the hope for relationships that nourish our souls. We yearn for those deep, meaningful connections—with our partners, our families, our friends, and even the people we work with. But if you're anything like I was, you might find that creating and nurturing those bonds isn't always easy. Perhaps you're caught in recurring patterns of miscommunication, struggle to express your needs, or feel a lingering disconnection, despite your best efforts. It can be disheartening, right? Believe me, I understand. I've walked that path, and I know how frustrating it can be to long for closeness yet feel like something is always getting in the way.

This book is born from that very struggle, from a deep desire to help others navigate the sometimes-turbulent waters of human connection. Think of it as a heartfelt conversation, a sharing of wisdom gleaned from years of experience, both personal and professional. Within these pages, we'll explore the intricacies of relationships, uncovering hidden dynamics that often trip us up. We'll explore practical, actionable strategies—tools you can use right away—to improve your communication, to set boundaries that honor both yourself and others, and to transform conflict from a source of pain into an opportunity for growth.

You see, so much of the wisdom we need is already within us, waiting to be uncovered. Sometimes, we just need a little guidance to see it clearly. Just as a mirror needs polishing to reflect truly, our hearts and minds sometimes need a gentle clearing away of old hurts, limiting beliefs, and ingrained patterns. That's what we'll do together. We'll explore how to build trust, cultivate vulnerability, and create a safe space for authentic connections to flourish.

This isn't about quick fixes or magic formulas. Instead, it's an unfolding journey of self-discovery and growth, one that promises more fulfilling and joyful relationships. And by learning to connect with yourself more deeply, you invite more authentic connections with others. Know that you're not alone in this. Many of us share these same struggles and longings. The path to deeper, more meaningful connections lies before you, and I'll be right here beside you, every step of the way. So, take a deep breath, open your heart, and let's begin.

No lover ever seeks union with his beloved,

But his beloved is also seeking union with him.

- Rumi

- Ahmed Mustafa

Chapter 1

THE RUSTY MIRROR

LOVE desires that this secret should be revealed,

For if a mirror reflects not, of what use is it?

Knowest thou why thy mirror reflects not?

Because the rust has not been scoured from its face.

If it were purified from all rust and defilement,

It would reflect the shining of the Sun of God.

– Rumi

Rumi asks a powerful question: "Why doesn't your mirror reflect clearly?" He's prompting us to look inside. He's saying that if we want to experience true love and connection, we need to clean the rust off our mirrors. Now, what does Rumi mean here? Think of it this way: we all want to love and be loved, to connect deeply with others, right? Rumi says that this deep connection, this love, is a secret that wants to be revealed. Our hearts are like mirrors. They're meant to reflect the best parts of ourselves and others. But sometimes, these mirrors get rusty. This "rust" is made up of all the old hurts, fears, and negative beliefs we carry around. Maybe you were hurt in the past, and now you're afraid to trust. Or maybe you learned to believe you weren't good enough, and now you push people away. This rust distorts the reflection, making it hard to see the good in ourselves and others, and making it hard to create healthy, loving connections.

In this first chapter, we'll explore those "rusty patterns"—their origins, their impact on our relationships, and the steps we can take to polish our inner mirrors. It's about learning to see ourselves and others more clearly to build the connections we truly long for. It's a path of self-discovery, and it all starts with looking into the mirror with kindness and a willingness to learn. This journey, though not always easy, is arguably the most important we can take. By understanding these patterns, we can begin to polish our inner mirrors. This allows our relationships to truly reflect who we are and the love we're capable of giving and receiving.

Relational Patterns

To illustrate the concept, let's turn to a story from Rumi's Masnavi. So, there were these two groups of painters, Chinese and Greek, who were always arguing about who was better. It was a long-standing rivalry, and nobody could really say which group was more talented. The Sultan, the king, got tired of all the bickering. He decided to have a contest to figure out who the best painters were. He gave each group a little house on his property, right across from each other. The Chinese painters asked for tons of colorful paints and got right to work, painting all sorts of beautiful designs on their walls. The Greek painters didn't ask for any paints. They just wanted some special stones for polishing. They spent their time scrubbing and polishing the walls of their house, getting rid of all the old dirt and making them super shiny.

The Chinese painters were focused on showcasing their skills, while the Greeks were quietly working away. Nobody knew what the Greeks were up to, not even the Chinese painters. Everyone was super excited to see what both groups had done.

After a month, it was time for the Sultan to judge. He went to the Chinese painters' house first and was blown away. They had transformed the little house into something extraordinary, dreamlike. It was really beautiful, and he had a hard time leaving.

Then, he went to the Greek painters' house. There was a big curtain in front of it. As the curtain was drawn back, the Sultan was astonished. The Greek painters had not painted a single stroke. Instead, they had polished the walls to such a degree that they became perfect mirrors. You could see the beautiful paintings from the Chinese house perfectly reflected on the walls.

It was like the Greek painters had taken the beauty of the Chinese paintings and made it even more stunning by reflecting it. The Sultan realized that the Greek painters had done something special. They showed that sometimes the best art is about finding the beauty that's already there and making it shine. They showed that simplicity can be just as powerful as a bunch of colors and designs.

This story serves as a powerful metaphor for our relationships: just as the Greek painters' bare walls revealed the true essence of the Chinese painters' art, our relationships illuminate our inner selves. They mirror both our strengths and weaknesses, offering a pathway to self-awareness and growth. The seemingly simple approach, like the Greeks' bare walls, can reveal concealed truths through reflection, much like relationships in our lives.

However, this analogy extends beyond a simple mirroring effect. The Greek painters did not copy the Chinese designs; instead, they provided a clear surface for the Chinese work to be seen in its enhanced form. This illustrates how relationships can help us understand ourselves by offering a space for reflection without distortion, revealing aspects of our inner world that may not be apparent otherwise. The relationship becomes a lens through which we see ourselves more clearly. They reflect back to us who we are, how we operate, and what we believe about ourselves and the world. The way you interact with your partner, your friends, your family—it all reveals something about your inner landscape. We often seek love and connection, driven by a deep-seated yearning to belong, but sometimes, what we see reflected in the mirror of our relationships isn't exactly what we expected or hoped for. Maybe you find yourself in similar relationship dynamics, over and over, that leave you feeling unfulfilled, confused, or even hurt. These recurring themes are what we call **relational patterns**.

These patterns are not random; they are often subconscious attempts to protect ourselves from perceived threats to connection, stemming from beliefs we've formed about our worthiness of love. Many times, these beliefs are rooted in our earliest experiences. Think of them as your default settings, the automatic responses you've developed over a lifetime. Like a smartphone that comes pre-loaded with certain apps and settings you didn't choose, your relational patterns are like pre-loaded software, influencing how you interact with others, often without you even realizing it. They operate in the background, shaping your expectations, behaviors, and emotional responses in relationships.

Attachment Theory

Attachment theory provides a valuable framework for understanding these patterns. It suggests that our early childhood experiences with our primary caregivers create an internal blueprint for how we relate to others throughout our lives. This blueprint shapes our expectations, our behaviors, and our emotional responses in relationships.

Consider this: If, as a child, you felt consistently loved, secure, and seen, you likely developed a **secure attachment style**. You tend to view relationships as a safe haven, and you're comfortable with both intimacy and independence. You trust that your needs will be met, and you're able to express them openly.

But what if your early experiences were different?

Perhaps you resonate with the **anxious-preoccupied style**. You might find yourself often feeling insecure in relationships, needing constant reassurance, and fearing abandonment. You might be drawn to partners who are emotionally unavailable, unconsciously recreating the dynamic of seeking love and approval from someone who can't fully give it.

Or maybe the **dismissive-avoidant style** feels more familiar. You might pride yourself on your independence, often prioritizing your own needs and goals above connection. You might find intimacy uncomfortable, and you tend to withdraw when things get too emotional. It's like preferring to work alone on a project, even when collaboration might be beneficial. You might fear that getting close to someone will mean losing your sense of self.

Then there's the **fearful-avoidant style**, a complex mix of both anxious and avoidant tendencies. You might crave intimacy but also fear it deeply, leading to a push-pull dynamic in relationships. You long for connection but also anticipate rejection, creating a self-fulfilling prophecy. It's like wanting to learn to swim but being terrified of the water.

It's important to keep in mind that these are general patterns, not rigid categories. Your personal attachment style might be a unique blend of these tendencies, and it can fluctuate across different relationships. The key is to see these styles not as fixed labels, but as potential lenses through which you view relationships.

And how do these attachment styles manifest in our relationships? They often show up as specific, and sometimes negative, patterns of behavior. For example:

- **The Rescuer:** You might be drawn to people who seem to need fixing, and you pour your energy into taking care of them, often neglecting your own needs in the process. This pattern might stem from a belief that you're only worthy of love if you're useful or needed, a belief that could be rooted in an anxious-preoccupied or fearful-avoidant attachment style where your own needs for care were not met consistently.

- **The Controller:** You might always need to be in charge, micromanaging your partner's life, and feeling **anxious** when things don't go your way. This could be a subconscious attempt to create a sense of safety and security, stemming from a fear of vulnerability or being out of control, which is common in avoidant attachment styles.

- **The Withdrawer:** You might avoid conflict like the plague, shutting down emotionally when things get tough, leaving your partner feeling isolated and abandoned. This pattern might be rooted in a fear of confrontation or a belief that expressing your needs will lead to rejection, a fear that can be linked to both anxious and avoidant attachment.

These tendencies offer valuable insights into your patterns, helping you understand why you react the way you do in certain situations, and ultimately, how you can begin to change those patterns for the better. And here's the key thing to understand: just like you can update or delete apps on your phone, you can update or rewrite your relational patterns. You might have developed them as a way to cope, to protect yourself, or to get your needs met in the past. But they don't define you as a whole.

Self-Discovery

As Eleanor Roosevelt wisely stated, "No one can make you feel inferior without your consent." This powerful statement underscores the importance of self-awareness in relationships. By understanding your attachment style and your relational patterns, you take back your power. You no longer have to be a passive recipient of your past programming. By illuminating these patterns, you create space for choice. You begin to shift from automatic reactions to conscious responses. You can choose to respond differently, to create new patterns, and to build healthier relationships.

Self-reflection involves honestly examining yourself, your patterns, and your behaviors. It means asking yourself tough questions and being willing to face the answers, even if they're uncomfortable. It's about realizing that the only person you can truly change is yourself. And it's about taking responsibility for your own growth and healing.

Journaling Prompts

Use these journaling prompts as a guide to your self-discovery:

- **Think about a recent conflict in a relationship.** What was your initial reaction? What pattern do you notice playing out?

- **Reflect on your early childhood.** What messages did you receive about love and relationships? How might those messages be influencing your current patterns?

- **Identify three significant relationships in your life.** What are the recurring themes or patterns you see in these connections?

- **Describe your ideal relationship.** What qualities does it possess? How do you behave in this ideal scenario?

- What is **one small step** you can take today to start shifting a negative pattern?

Self-awareness is the key that unlocks your relational potential. When you understand why you do what you do, you can begin to make conscious choices about how you want to behave in the future. It's like learning to dance. At first, you might stumble, step on your partner's toes, or feel awkward. But with practice, you learn the steps, you find your rhythm, and you begin to move with greater ease and grace. You become more attuned to your partner, more responsive to their needs, and more confident in your own movements.

Changing your relational patterns takes time, effort, and a willingness to be vulnerable. It requires you to step outside of your comfort zone, to try new things, and to risk being seen for who you truly are. While this process may present challenges, the rewards are immeasurable. **Healthier relationships, greater intimacy, deeper connection, and a more fulfilling life are all within your reach.** When we clear away the rust through self-awareness and comprehension, that inner light can shine through, and our relationships can reflect that brilliance. This is the essence of Rumi's "shining of the Sun of God"—your inner light, your true self, the loving, joyful, and remarkable individual that resides at your core.

Key Takeaways

- **Your Relationships Reflect You:** Your relationships act as mirrors, reflecting your inner world and revealing your deeply ingrained patterns.

- **Early Experiences Shape Patterns:** Your early childhood experiences shaped your attachment style, which significantly influences your relationship patterns.

- **Awareness is Power:** Recognizing your patterns—like "The Rescuer," "The Controller," or "The Withdrawer"—is the crucial first step towards changing them. You gain the power to choose your responses when you understand why you react the way you do.

- **You Can Change:** You are not defined by your past. You have the power to rewrite your relational patterns and create healthier, more fulfilling connections.

- **Self-Reflection is Key:** Honest self-reflection, like polishing a rusty mirror as Rumi said, allows you to see yourself clearly and create relationships that reflect your true self and your capacity for love.

∼

Chapter 2

WORDS THAT HEAL

Every expression is the sign of a state of mind;

That state is a hand, the expression an instrument.

A goldsmith's instruments in the hand of a cobbler

Are as grains of wheat sown on sand.

For he who is ignorant misuses the instrument;

If you strike flint on mud you will get no fire.

— Rumi

Rumi's wisdom illuminates the deep connection between our inner state and our outward expression, particularly in how we communicate. He suggests that our words and actions are merely "instruments" wielded by the "hand" of our inner state — our emotions, intentions, and beliefs. If our inner state is clouded by negativity, fear, or a lack of awareness, our communication will likely be ineffective, like a "cobbler" trying to use a "goldsmith's instruments." Similarly, striking "flint on mud" produces no spark. If we are "ignorant" of our own inner state, if we are not mindful of our emotions and intentions, our attempts at communication will probably miss the mark. This chapter is about cultivating the inner state that allows us to use the tools of compassionate communication effectively, transforming our interactions from mere exchanges of words to heartfelt dialogues that nourish our relationships and enrich our lives. This involves learning to speak not just from the mind, but from the heart—igniting the spark of understanding, even in challenging conversations.

Think about the people who have truly touched your heart. What was it about their way of communicating that made you feel seen, heard, and understood? Chances are, they spoke with compassion, genuinely desiring to connect with your inner world. They listened not just to your words, but to the emotions behind them. They spoke their truth with kindness and respect. **That's the essence of compassionate communication.**

The Quran emphasizes the importance of speaking with kindness and respect, stating:

"And say to My slaves (i.e. believers) that they should (only) say those words that are the best."

(Surah Al-Isra, 17:53)

This verse reminds us of the power of our words—they can heal or wound, build up or tear down. Compassionate communication is about choosing our words wisely, intending to foster understanding and connection. It's about recognizing that every interaction is an opportunity to either strengthen or weaken our relationships.

Prophet Muhammad (P.B.U.H) said:

"He who believes in Allah and the Last Day should either utter good words or better keep silence; and he who believes in Allah and the Last Day should treat his neighbor with kindness and he who believes in Allah and the Last Day should show hospitality to his guest." (Sahih Muslim 47a)

Some people asked Prophet Muhammad (P.B.U.H), "Whose Islam is the best? i.e. (Who is a very good Muslim)?" He replied, "One who avoids harming the Muslims with his tongue and hands." (Sahih al-Bukhari 11)

These teachings highlight the immense emphasis the Prophet (P.B.U.H) placed on communication. He stressed that our words should always embody kindness and refrain from causing harm to the listener in any manner. This principle extends beyond mere politeness; it involves deep consideration for the impact of our words on others' emotional and spiritual well-being. It calls for a mindful awareness of the potential for even seemingly innocuous words to cause unintentional pain or offense. True compassionate communication, as exemplified by the Prophet (P.B.U.H), is rooted in empathy, respect, and a genuine concern for the well-being of others.

Let's ponder on a story from Rumi's Masnavi:

It was getting late, and a shepherd was bringing his goats home. He was in a great mood, thinking about how nice the cool evening would be. He started praising God, saying things like, "Where are you, my dear God? I want to fix your shoes, comb your hair, wash your clothes, and even pick the lice out of your hair! I'll bring you milk and rub your tired feet. You're my everything, and all my goats are yours." He was just expressing his love in his own simple way.

Now, the Prophet Moses happened to be nearby and heard all this. When the shepherd was done, Moses, sounding very serious, asked him, "Who were you talking to like that?" The shepherd, not realizing who Moses was, innocently replied, "The one who made us all, the earth and sky."

Moses got really upset and said, "What are you talking about? I'm Moses, the prophet, and you need to stop saying such words! God doesn't have a body or wear shoes. He doesn't need milk. Your words don't make any sense!" The shepherd was shocked and felt terrible. He said, "Oh, Moses, you've shut me up! I'm so sorry." He tore his shirt, threw it away, and ran off crying into the desert.

Later, Moses fell into a deep sleep and had a dream. He heard God's voice, which said, "Moses, what did you do? You pushed away my loyal servant! I sent you to bring people closer to me, not to push them away. Everyone has their own way of praying. It doesn't matter what words they use, it's what's in their heart that counts. I want to see the fire of love in their souls!"

When Moses woke up, he felt completely different. He realized and went to find the shepherd. He followed the shepherd's strange footprints, which showed how upset he had been. Eventually, Moses found him and gently said, "God himself has blessed you! He told me I was wrong to be so critical of you. He loves your simple prayers from the heart. You can keep praying just like you always have."

But the shepherd had changed. He looked different, and his voice was deeper. He told Moses, "I've gone way beyond the words now. I've traveled far in my soul, thanks to you. I've traveled past the earth and the sky, a thousand years beyond! Your words woke me up. I don't even know who I am anymore. All I know is that I'm sailing away, but where to, I cannot tell." Then, the shepherd said goodbye and walked off into the desert, disappearing from sight. He was on a different journey now, the right way to communicate with the divine.

In this story, the shepherd's prayer symbolizes honest, heartfelt communication unique to each individual, emphasizing that different people express themselves differently. God's guidance to Moses highlights the need for empathy, understanding, and valuing the spirit behind the communication, showing that true compassionate communication involves seeing beyond superficial differences. This narrative reveals that compassionate communication is not simply about using kind words, but about realizing, respecting, and valuing the unique ways in which individuals express themselves, while also being open to personal transformation through the communication itself.

The Importance of Nonverbal Communication

It's important to understand that communication is more than just the words we use. **It's the tone of our voice, the expression on our face, the posture of our body.** It's the energy we bring to the interaction, the intention behind our words. It's like a dance, a delicate interplay between two souls. And just like any dance, it requires practice, skill, and a willingness to be present with your partner.

Here's where things get tricky. Sometimes, our verbal and nonverbal cues are mismatched. Nonverbal cues play a pivotal role in the reception of our messages. Consider this: For example, you can say "I'm fine," but if your voice is trembling, your eyes are downcast, and your shoulders are slumped, the other person will likely sense that something is wrong. You might say "Yes, I'm listening," while simultaneously checking your phone. This sends a mixed message, leaving the other person feeling confused and unimportant. Or, you might say, "I'm not angry" in a tight, clipped tone with a furrowed brow, which clearly contradicts your words. Our bodies often speak a truth that our words try to conceal.

Paying attention to your nonverbal cues is just as essential as choosing your words carefully. Are you making eye contact? Is your posture open and receptive? Are your facial expressions aligned with what you're saying? These subtle cues dramatically affect how your message is received.

Four Pillars of Compassionate Communication

So, how do we master this language of the heart? How do we move beyond the superficial exchange of words and create truly meaningful connections? As we touched upon in the previous chapter, self-awareness is key. That same awareness can be expanded to encompass these four pillars of compassionate communication. Let's explore some practical techniques:

1. Mindful Presence: Instead of just "being present," let's get specific. Here's how to truly be present in a conversation:

- Put away distractions: This is a simple but powerful step. Make a conscious effort to remove anything that might pull your attention away from the person you're talking to. Turn off your laptop, silence your phone, and put it facedown.

- Make eye contact: Look at the person you're talking to. This doesn't mean staring intensely, but maintaining a natural level of eye contact that shows you're engaged. It's a nonverbal way of saying, "I'm here with you."

- Listen to understand, not to respond: This is a crucial distinction. Often, when we're listening to someone, we're already formulating our response in our heads. Instead, try to quiet your inner voice and focus solely on what the other person is saying. Try to understand their perspective, their feelings, and their needs.

- Notice nonverbal cues: Pay attention to the person's body language, their tone of voice, and their facial expressions. These cues often convey more than their words alone. For example, a furrowed brow might indicate concern, even if they're saying they're fine.

- Resist the urge to interrupt: Let the person finish their thoughts before jumping in with your own. Interrupting, cutting them off mid-sentence, or preventing them from fully expressing themselves, can make someone feel unheard and disrespected.

Real-life examples:

- Scenario 1: Your partner is telling you about a difficult day at work. Instead of glancing at your phone while they're talking, you put it away, make eye contact, and focus on their words and emotions. You nod along to show you're listening and resist the urge to offer solutions until they've finished expressing themselves.

- **Scenario 2:** Your friend is sharing exciting news about a new project. Instead of thinking about what you're going to say next, you focus on their excitement, mirroring their enthusiasm with your facial expressions and asking follow-up questions to show your genuine interest.

- **Scenario 3:** During a disagreement with a family member, instead of mentally rehearsing your counter-arguments, you make a conscious effort to listen to their perspective. You maintain eye contact, even when it's difficult, and try to understand the emotions or care behind their words.

2. Empathy: Empathy is not merely a passive feeling; it is a skill that can be cultivated and honed through practice. It involves stepping into the other person's shoes, trying to understand their perspective, and connecting with their feelings, even if you don't necessarily agree with their actions or viewpoint. Here are some practical tools to strengthen this skill:

- Reflect and Summarize: As we touched upon earlier, summarizing what you heard is a great starting point. It shows you're paying attention and making an effort to understand. For example, "What I hear you saying is that you felt hurt when

I didn't call you back yesterday. Is that right?" This gives the other person a chance to confirm or clarify their feelings.

- Acknowledge and Validate Emotions: Go beyond just summarizing the content of what they said. Name the emotions you think they might be feeling and validate their experience. For instance, "That sounds incredibly frustrating," or "I can understand why you'd feel disappointed." Even if you wouldn't react the same way in a similar situation, acknowledging their feelings as valid is crucial for building a connection.

- Ask Open-Ended Questions: Encourage the person to share more about their experience. Questions like, "Can you tell me more about that?" or "How did that make you feel?" show that you're genuinely interested in understanding their perspective.

- Imagine Yourself in Their Shoes: This is the core of empathy. Try to truly imagine what it would be like to be in the other person's situation, considering their background, experiences, and personality. Ask yourself, "How would I feel if that happened to me?"

- Listen for Unmet Needs: Often, behind strong emotions lie unmet needs. Try to identify what the person might be needing at that moment. Are they seeking love, validation, support, or something else?

Real-Life Examples:

- **Scenario 1:** Your friend is upset because he/she didn't get the promotion he/she was hoping for. Instead of saying, "Don't worry, you'll get it next time," you could say, "That sounds really disappointing. You worked so hard for that promotion. It's understandable that you'd feel upset. Is there anything I can do to support you?"

- **Scenario 2:** Your partner is expressing frustration about a conflict with their sibling. Instead of offering advice on how to fix the situation, you could say, "Family conflicts can be so draining. It sounds like you're feeling really hurt and frustrated by what happened. What do you think you need right now?"

- **Scenario 3:** Your child is acting out, and instead of immediately scolding them, take a moment to consider what might be behind their behavior. Ask yourself if they are tired, hungry, or feeling overwhelmed. You might discover that they are acting out because they need attention or a hug.

Why is empathy so valuable in compassionate communication?

Empathy creates a sense of connection and understanding. When someone feels seen and heard, they're more likely to open up and be receptive to your perspective. It diffuses defensiveness and creates a space for collaboration and problem-solving. It's the bridge that allows us to connect with others on a deeper, more meaningful level. By practicing these techniques, you can develop your empathy muscles and build stronger, more compassionate relationships.

3. Authenticity: This means speaking your truth, but with kindness and respect. It's about being real, being genuine, and expressing yourself in a way that is both clear and kind. One powerful technique for expressing yourself authentically is to use **"I" statements.** This means taking ownership of your feelings and experiences, rather than blaming or accusing the other person.

Here are some more examples:

- Instead of: "You never listen to me." Try: "I feel unheard when I share my feelings, and I need to know that you're listening."

- Instead of: "You're always late." Try: "I feel frustrated when you're late because it throws off my schedule, and I value punctuality."

- Instead of: "You never help around the house." Try: "I feel overwhelmed when I have to do all the chores by myself, and I need your help to balance the workload."

"I" statements help to de-escalate conflict and create a more collaborative atmosphere. They allow you to express your needs and feelings without making the other person defensive.

4. Non-Judgment: Approach conversations with an open mind, suspending judgment, and trying to understand their perspective. This can be challenging, especially when you strongly disagree with someone or feel hurt by their actions. But let's not forget, judgment creates barriers to connection, while understanding builds bridges. It involves recognizing that everyone is doing the best they can with what they have, given their unique circumstances, experiences, and beliefs. It doesn't mean condoning harmful behavior, but rather striving to understand the underlying motivations and perspectives.

Here's how to cultivate a non-judgmental approach:

- Challenge Your Assumptions: We all make assumptions about others, often based on limited information. When you find yourself judging someone, pause and ask yourself, "What assumptions am I making? What else might be going on that I'm not aware of?"

- Practice Perspective-Taking: Make a conscious effort to see things from the other person's point of view. This doesn't mean you have to agree with them, but it can help you understand where they're coming from. Ask yourself, "Why might they have acted that way?"

- Separate the Person from the Behavior: Be mindful that a person's actions don't necessarily define who they are. Someone might make a mistake or act in a way you disapprove of, but that doesn't make them inherently "bad." Try to separate the behavior from the person.

- Focus on Understanding, Not Agreement: The goal is not to agree with everyone, but to understand their perspective. You can still hold different opinions while maintaining respect for the other person's right to their viewpoint.

- Be Mindful of Your Inner Critic: We often judge others in the same way we judge ourselves. If you tend to be hard on yourself, you might be more likely to judge others harshly as well. Practice self-compassion, and extend that same compassion to others.

Real-Life Examples:

- Scenario 1: A coworker makes a mistake on an important project. Instead of thinking, "They're so incompetent," you could remind yourself that everyone makes mistakes and try to understand what might have contributed to the error. Perhaps they were under a lot of pressure, or they didn't have the necessary resources to give their best.

- Scenario 2: A friend expresses a political opinion that you strongly disagree with. Instead of labeling them as "ignorant" or "misguided," you could try to understand the experiences and values that have shaped their beliefs. You can still disagree with their opinion while respecting their right to hold it.

- **Scenario 3:** Your partner snaps at you after a long day. Instead of assuming they're just being mean, you could consider that they might be stressed, tired, or overwhelmed. You could ask, "You seem stressed. Is everything okay?"

Why being non-judgmental is crucial for compassionate communication?

When you approach conversations with a non-judgmental attitude, you create a safe space for the other person to express themselves honestly. They're more likely to feel comfortable sharing their thoughts and feelings without fear of being criticized or rejected. This openness fosters deeper understanding and strengthens the connection between you. It allows for a more authentic and productive exchange, even when discussing difficult topics.

As John Gottman, a renowned relationship researcher, wisely said,

"In the strongest relationships, people express their needs and work together to find solutions that work for both of them."

It's a course of continuous learning, growth, and refinement. There will be times when you stumble, when you say things you later regret. That's perfectly acceptable. It's an inherent part of the process. The key is to keep practicing and striving to communicate with compassion.

Key Takeaways

- **Your Inner State Shapes Your Words:** Your emotions and intentions significantly influence how you communicate. A compassionate inner state leads to compassionate communication.

- **Compassion is Key:** Speak and listen from the heart, choosing words that foster understanding and connection. Kindness and empathy are paramount.

- **Listen to Understand:** Truly listen to others, not just to respond. Pay attention to their words, emotions, and nonverbal cues. Practice empathy by trying to see things from their perspective.

- **Use "I" Statements:** Express your feelings and needs authentically and respectfully by using "I" statements. This helps you take ownership of your experience without blaming others.

- **Suspend Judgment:** Approach conversations with an open mind, seeking to understand rather than to judge. Take into account that everyone is doing their best based on their own experiences and perspectives.

∼

Chapter 3

GUARDING THE TEMPLE

When the body bows in worship, the heart is a temple,

And where there is a temple, there bad friends are weeds.

When a liking for bad friends grows up in you,

Flee from them, and avoid converse with them.

Root up those weeds, for, if they attain full growth,

They will subvert you and your temple together.

— Rumi

In these evocative lines, Rumi uses the metaphor of the heart as a "temple" to emphasize the importance of safeguarding our inner sanctuary. He suggests that just as a temple requires protection from those who would defile it, our hearts need boundaries to protect us from negative influences. "Bad friends," in this context, can be interpreted as any relationships or influences that drain our energy, disrespect our values, or undermine our well-being. They are the "weeds" that threaten to choke the growth of our inner peace and self-respect.

Rumi urges us to be vigilant, to recognize when these negative influences are taking root, and to take decisive action to "flee" from them. This isn't about being unkind or judgmental, but about recognizing not all connections are healthy for us. Just as a gardener must diligently weed their garden for plants to flourish, we must establish boundaries to protect our inner temple. This chapter is about learning to identify those "weeds"—the unhealthy relationships and patterns that violate our boundaries—and developing the skills to "root them up" so that our hearts can remain a sacred space where healthy connections can thrive. Essentially, setting boundaries is an act of self-love, a way of honoring the sanctity of our own inner temple.

Let's be honest: **setting boundaries can be really tough.** It can trigger all sorts of fears — fear of rejection, fear of conflict, fear of being seen as selfish or unloving. We worry that if we say "no," we'll damage our relationships, disappoint others, or even end up alone. These fears are often rooted in those early attachment patterns we explored in Chapter 1, where we may have learned that our needs are less important than the needs of others.

The Qur'an states,

"O believers! Do not enter any house other than your own until you have asked for permission and greeted its occupants. This is best for you, so perhaps you will be mindful."

(Surah An-Nur, 24:27)

This verse from the Quran, while literally about physical boundaries and respecting privacy, can be interpreted metaphorically as a foundational principle for establishing boundaries in various aspects of life. It emphasizes the importance of seeking consent and respecting the "space" of others, whether it be physical, emotional, or mental.

Extending this concept, we can see that healthy boundaries are essential for maintaining harmonious relationships. Just as entering someone's home without permission is a violation, so is intruding upon someone's emotional space without invitation or sensitivity. This includes respecting their right to their feelings, thoughts, and time. By acknowledging and honoring these boundaries, we demonstrate respect and create an environment where individuals feel safe and valued.

The Quran further emphasizes the concept of boundaries in interpersonal relationships by advising believers to speak kindly and avoid gossip or backbiting,

"O believers! Avoid many suspicions, 'for' indeed, some suspicions are sinful. And do not spy, nor backbite one another.

(Surah Al-Hujurat, 49:12).

This highlights the importance of setting boundaries in our communication, ensuring that our words are respectful and do not infringe upon the dignity of others. It also speaks about setting digital boundaries. In an age dominated by digital communication, the verse can be interpreted as a reminder to be mindful of our online interactions. It encourages us to seek consent before sharing personal information about others, to be respectful in our online communication, and to be mindful of the boundaries between our online and offline lives. It involves achieving a delicate equilibrium between honoring our individual needs and nurturing healthy, respectful relationships.

Prophet Muhammad (P.B.U.H) said: "He who peeped into the house of people without their consent, it is permissible for them to put out his eyes." (Sahih Muslim 2158a)

This hadith underscores the gravity with which Islam views the violation of privacy and personal boundaries. It serves as a powerful metaphor for the importance of respecting personal space and the sanctity of one's private life. In a broader sense, this hadith can be interpreted as emphasizing the right to protect oneself from any form of intrusion, whether physical, emotional, or psychological. It highlights the principle that individuals have the right to defend their boundaries and that violating those boundaries has consequences. This teaching reinforces the idea that personal boundaries are not merely a matter of preference but are fundamental to maintaining one's dignity and well-being. It's a reminder that we are entitled to set limits on what we are willing to tolerate from others and to take steps to protect ourselves from harm, otherwise, as Rumi said, *"They will subvert you and your temple together."*

Think of boundaries as the invisible lines that define where you end and another person begins. They're not walls meant to keep people out, but rather fences that create a safe and respectful space for you to interact with others. They allow you to maintain your sense of self while connecting with others.

Types of Boundaries

Let's explore the different types of boundaries through practical examples:

1. Physical Boundaries:

This is about your personal space and physical touch. It's your right to decide who touches you, how they touch you, and when. Understanding and respecting physical boundaries is fundamental to feeling safe and comfortable in any interaction.

Example: You have an acquaintance who greets you with a hug, however, you aren't comfortable with this level of physical touch. You can set a boundary by saying,

"It's nice to see you, but I'm not really a hugger. A handshake is great."

Enforcing it: If someone tries to hug you anyway, you might gently step back and reiterate, "As I mentioned, I prefer a handshake." You can also add a brief explanation if you feel comfortable, such as, "I just feel more comfortable with a little more personal space." Remember, you don't owe anyone a detailed explanation of your boundaries, but sometimes a simple clarification can help.

2. Emotional Boundaries:

This is about protecting your feelings and emotional energy. It's your right to choose what emotional experiences you share with others and how much you engage with their emotions. Healthy emotional boundaries allow you to be empathetic without becoming overwhelmed by other people's feelings.

Example: A friend constantly complains about their problems, leaving you feeling drained. A good way to set a boundary is to say, "I care about you, and I want to be supportive, but I'm finding it difficult to listen to these complaints all the time. Can we also talk about some positive things happening in your life?"

Enforcing it: If the friend continues to only complain, you might say, "I'm feeling overwhelmed by negativity right now. I need to take a break from this conversation, but I'm happy to connect later and talk about something else." You can also add, "I'm starting to feel emotionally depleted, and I need to protect my own energy." Be certain that it's okay to prioritize your emotional well-being, even in close relationships.

3. Mental Boundaries:

This is about your thoughts, values, and opinions. It's your right to have your own beliefs and to think independently, without being subjected to pressure or criticism. Protecting your mental boundaries means maintaining your intellectual autonomy and not allowing others to dictate what you should think or believe.

Example: A family member often makes critical remarks about your life choices. Boundaries could be set by saying, "I appreciate your concern, but I'm confident in my decisions. I'd appreciate it if you would respect my choices, even if you don't agree with them."

Enforcing it: If the family member continues to criticize, you might say, "As I mentioned, I'm not looking for your approval on this. Let's change the subject." You can further reinforce this by saying, "My choices are based on my values and goals, and I'm not willing to debate them." It's imperative to stand firm in your beliefs and not allow others to undermine your confidence.

4. Material Boundaries:

This is about your possessions and finances. It's your right to decide how your belongings are used and how your money is spent. Setting material boundaries helps prevent resentment and ensures that your resources are used in a way that aligns with your values and priorities.

Example: A coworker keeps borrowing money and not paying you back. You might set a boundary by saying, "I'm not comfortable lending money anymore. I hope you understand."

Enforcing it: If the coworker asks to borrow money again, you can say, "As I said, I'm not lending money at the moment." You might add, "I need to make sure I'm managing my finances responsibly." Don't forget, you have no obligation to share your resources with others if it makes you uncomfortable or creates a hardship for you.

5. Time Boundaries:

This is about how you spend your time and energy.

Example: You're a people-pleaser who struggles to say "no" to requests, leaving you feeling over-committed and exhausted. Setting a boundary might involve saying, "I'd love to help, but I'm already committed to other things right now. I can't take on that extra task."

Enforcing it: If someone tries to pressure you, you might say, "I understand this is important, but as I explained, my schedule is full. I need to prioritize my existing commitments."

Consistency is key to training others how to treat you. Setting boundaries requires effort and a willingness to reinforce your limits each time they are tested. It is not about elevating oneself over others, but about maintaining the self-respect and dignity that is essential for healthy relationships. It involves honoring your worth and teaching others to do the same.

Here are some effective strategies for enforcing boundaries:

Be Assertive, Not Aggressive: Use the "I" statements we learned in Chapter 2 to communicate your needs clearly and respectfully, without blaming or attacking the other person. This approach allows you to express your feelings and stand your ground without escalating the conflict.

Stay Calm and Firm: Even when facing resistance, maintain your composure. Don't give in to guilt or pressure. You have a right to your boundaries. Your feelings and needs are valid, and you deserve to have them respected.

Anticipate Objections: Think about how the other person might react and prepare your responses beforehand. This will help you stay firm in your resolve. By mentally rehearsing different scenarios, you'll feel more confident and less likely to be caught off guard.

Don't Over-Explain: You don't need to justify your boundaries or provide lengthy explanations. A simple and direct statement is often more effective. Over-explaining can sometimes weaken your position and invite unnecessary debate.

Be prepared to walk away if necessary: If someone repeatedly violates your boundaries and refuses to respect them, you may need to distance yourself from the relationship, at least temporarily. This is not about punishing the other person, but about protecting your own well-being.

Self-Boundaries

It's equally important to set boundaries with yourself too. Self-boundaries are commitments made to protect well-being and prevent self-sabotage, a form of self-discipline that helps you stay aligned with your values and goals. By setting and maintaining self-boundaries, you create a sense of inner structure and stability, which can improve your self-esteem and overall quality of life.

Here are some examples of self-boundaries:

- "I will not engage in negative self-talk. I will treat myself with the same kindness and compassion that I offer others."

- "I will not stay up past midnight on weeknights, so I can get enough rest."

- "I will not check my work email after 6 PM to maintain a healthy work-life balance."

- "I will not spend more than 30 minutes a day on social media, to avoid getting caught in the comparison trap."

Establishing these boundaries is an act of self-love. It's a way of saying, "I value myself enough to protect my time, energy, and well-being." It's not about being rigid or inflexible, but about making conscious choices that support your needs and goals.

As renowned psychologist and author Henry Cloud wisely stated, "Boundaries define us. They define what is me and what is not me. A boundary shows me where I end, and someone else begins, leading me to a sense of ownership."

This quote beautifully highlights that boundaries are not just about what we allow from others, but also about what we allow from ourselves. They help us define our values, our priorities, and our limits. They empower us to take ownership of our lives, our choices, and our well-being. By setting boundaries with ourselves, we create an internal framework that guides our actions and helps us stay true to our authentic selves.

Take into account the communication skills we explored in Chapter 2—they are your allies in this process. Specifically, using "I" statements and practicing active listening can help you articulate your boundaries with clarity and empathy. These tools will empower you to express your needs without blame or aggression, fostering understanding and respect in your relationships. By combining compassionate communication with clear boundaries, you create a foundation for relationships that are both fulfilling and empowering. Additionally, setting boundaries allows you to conserve your energy for the people and activities that truly matter to you, leading to a more meaningful and purposeful life. When you respect your own limits, you also teach others to respect them, creating a positive cycle of mutual understanding and consideration. Keep practicing and as Rumi said, *"Root up those weeds"*. You've got this!

Key Takeaways

- **Boundaries are Essential for Well-being:** Boundaries are not walls, but rather healthy guidelines that define your needs and limits, protecting your physical, emotional, and mental well-being. They are essential for both self-respect and healthy relationships.

- **Your Heart is a Temple:** Like Rumi's metaphor of the heart as a temple, you must guard your inner self against **negative** influences ("weeds") that drain your energy or disrespect your values.

- **Boundaries are an Act of Self-Love:** Setting and enforcing boundaries is a way of honoring your own needs and demonstrating self-respect. It's about saying, "I value myself enough to protect my well-being." This includes setting boundaries with yourself.

- **Consistency is Key:** Setting a boundary once is not enough. Consistently enforcing your boundaries teaches others how to treat you and reinforces your commitment to your well-being.

- **You Have a Right to Protect Yourself:** You have the right to set boundaries in all areas of your life—physical, emotional, mental, material, and time. If someone repeatedly violates your boundaries, it's okay to distance yourself to protect your well-being, as supported by the teachings of the Quran and Prophet Muhammad (P.B.U.H).

~

Chapter 4

FROM EGO TO EMPATHY

In fine, outward actions are guides

To show the way to what is concealed within.

Sometimes the guide is true, sometimes false,

Sometimes a help, and at other times a hindrance.

Though reality is exposed to view in this form,

Form is at once nigh to and far from reality.

For instance, these two resemble water and a tree;

When you look to their essence they are far apart;

Yet see how quickly a seed becomes a high tree

Out of water, along with earth and sunshine!

— Rumi

In these insightful verses, Rumi explores the complex relationship between our inner world and our outward actions, a dynamic that is particularly relevant when navigating conflict. He suggests that while our actions can serve as "guides" to our inner state, they can also be misleading. Just as a "guide" can be "true" or "false," our outward expressions during conflict may not always accurately reflect our true intentions or underlying needs. Sometimes, our actions are a "help," leading to realization and resolution. Other times, they can be a "hindrance," escalating the conflict and obscuring the path to harmony.

Rumi uses the analogy of a tree and water to illustrate this duality. On the surface, they appear vastly different, yet water is essential for the tree's growth. Similarly, in situations of conflict, seemingly opposing perspectives may be interconnected, and understanding the underlying needs—the "water" that nourishes each perspective—is crucial for growth and resolution. This chapter is about learning to discern between the "true" and "false" guides in conflict, to see beyond the surface of outward actions, and to understand the deeper needs that fuel them. Like the seed that needs water and earth, conflict can be a catalyst for growth and deeper connection if we navigate it with grace and empathy. Just as the right conditions are necessary for a seed to grow into a tree, the right approach to dealing with conflict will create harmony.

Understanding Conflict

Conflict, in its essence, is simply a difference in needs, desires, or perspectives. It's not inherently bad or good. It just is. It's a natural part of being human and interacting with other humans. We are, after all, unique individuals with our own thoughts, feelings, and experiences. But how we *respond* to conflict makes all the difference.

The Quran encourages believers to resolve their disputes amicably, stating:

"The believers are but brothers, so make settlement between your brothers. And fear Allah that you may receive mercy."

(Surah Al-Hujurat, 49:10).

This verse highlights the importance of maintaining harmony within the community and resolving conflicts in a way that is pleasing to God. It's a reminder that even in disagreement, we are still connected. This teaches us to approach conflict resolution with a spirit of brotherhood, seeking to understand each other's perspectives and find common ground. It encourages empathy, forgiveness, and a willingness to compromise for the sake of unity.

The Qur'an further prohibits us to not ridicule others by offensive nicknames whether in a conflict or not,

"O believers! Do not let some 'men' ridicule others, they may be better than them, nor let 'some' women ridicule other women, they may be better than them. Do not defame one another, nor call each other by offensive nicknames."

(Surah Al-Hujurat, 49:11)

Prophet Muhammad (peace be upon him) said, "He who is not merciful to others will not be treated mercifully." (Sahih al-Bukhari 6013).

This hadith underscores the vital role of empathy in our interactions. When we approach others with compassion and empathy, particularly during challenging conversations, we create a space for genuine connection and mutual respect. It's a reminder that our actions towards others often mirror the treatment we receive in return. This principle encourages us to break the cycle of negativity and to respond to conflict with kindness. By extending mercy to others, we not only foster a more harmonious environment but also open ourselves to receiving mercy in return.

There's a beautiful story of Imam Ali in Rumi's Masnavi that highlights the necessity of pausing and refraining from impulsive reactions when conflict arises:

In the early days of Islam, there were many battles fought in the region of Arabia. In one of these battles, Ali, the

Prophet Muhammad's (P.B.U.H) son-in-law and a skilled warrior, was fighting a strong opponent. Ali quickly defeated him and was about to kill him. The defeated soldier, thinking it was his last moment, spat in Ali's face as a final act of defiance.

But then, something unexpected happened. Ali lowered his sword and walked away, sparing the man's life. The soldier was shocked and confused. He called out to Ali, "Why did you stop? You were about to kill me. What changed your mind? You had won, so why didn't you finish me off?"

Ali explained, "I only fight for God. I'm his servant, not fighting for myself. I'm God's lion, not some warrior driven by his feelings. My actions, not my words, show what I believe in. Even though I hold the sword, it's God who decides when to strike. Just like the wind can't move a mountain, I won't act unless it's God's will."

He continued, "Anger reigns over most kings, but I control my anger. It's my patience that sets me free from anger's grip. My sword doesn't just kill; it can also give life. When you spat at me, you made it personal. It wasn't about God anymore. My ego got involved, and my anger flared up. If I had killed you then, it would have been half for God and half for my own ego. That's why I stopped."

Then, Ali turned and walked away, leaving the soldier alive and pondering the deeper meaning of Ali's actions. Ali showed that true strength isn't just about winning a fight, but about controlling your emotions and acting according to your principles, even when provoked. He also wanted to teach us that fighting for a cause should be selfless, if you bring your ego to a holy war, then it is not holy anymore.

This remarkable act of Imam Ali serves as a tangible illustration of the Prophet Muhammad's (peace be upon him) saying:

"The strong is not the one who overcomes the people by his strength, but the strong is the one who controls himself while in anger." (Sahih al-Bukhari 6114).

This story is a powerful example of navigating conflict gracefully. It highlights the importance of pausing to consider a thoughtful response, rather than reacting impulsively from emotion. The act of Imam Ali guides us to identify the conflict's true nature, setting aside personal ego and focusing on the underlying problem. This approach requires us to manage our emotions, especially anger, to achieve a more effective and harmonious outcome. Ultimately, a higher purpose can serve as our compass, guiding us through the storm of conflict and helping us rise above petty disagreements.

Shifting from Ego to Empathy

Often, when conflict arises, our ego takes the driver's seat. The ego is that part of us that's concerned with being right, with winning, with protecting our sense of self-worth at all costs. It's the part that wants to defend, attack, or withdraw. It's like a little voice inside our heads that says, "I need to win this argument," or "I need to prove that I'm right." But as we learned in our exploration of self-awareness, the ego is not the true self.

So, how do we shift from ego to empathy?

The first step is recognizing when our ego is triggered. Often, it's the other person's words that set us off. Certain phrases or tones of voice can feel like a personal attack, even if that wasn't the intention. For example, phrases like "You always..." or "You never..." can instantly put us on the defensive. These types of statements often feel like accusations, triggering our ego's need to protect itself. When we feel attacked, our ego wants to jump in and defend, retaliate, or shut down. This is where we get caught in a cycle of conflict, with both parties reacting from their egos rather than responding with empathy.

Here's a practical exercise to facilitate that crucial shift: Before reacting to a perceived attack, pause and take a deep breath. In that pause, ask yourself, "What might be the other person's underlying need or perspective? What unmet need might be driving their behavior? What emotions might they be experiencing that are causing them to express themselves in this way?"

For example, if your partner snaps at you for being late, instead of reacting defensively ("I'm only a few minutes late, what's the big deal?"), try to consider what might be behind their frustration. Maybe they're feeling stressed about work, and your lateness added to their stress. Or perhaps they were looking forward to spending quality time with you, and your tardiness felt like a disregard for their feelings. They might be feeling hurt, disappointed, or even disrespected, and those feelings are getting expressed as anger.

Try to listen beyond the words and hear the underlying emotion. Think of the active listening techniques from Chapter 2—paying attention to tone of voice and body language can provide valuable clues. Instead of focusing on the perceived attack, focus on the underlying need that's not being met. This shift in perspective allows you to respond with empathy rather than defensiveness. It allows you to address the root cause of the conflict, rather than getting caught up in a superficial argument. By realizing the underlying need, you can move from a place of defensiveness to a place of understanding and connection. You can start to see the other person not as an adversary, but as a human being with their own struggles and vulnerabilities.

Handling Emotional Escalation

When conversations get heated, it's easy to fall back into old, unhelpful patterns. This is where we can leverage the self-awareness we cultivated in Chapter 1. Identifying your triggers—those situations or topics that tend to provoke a strong emotional response—is the first step. However, it's equally crucial to recognize when the other person is becoming triggered. Are they raising their voice? Are they becoming defensive? These are signs that the conversation is heading in an unproductive direction.

When you sense tension rising, consider these steps:

1. **Acknowledge Your Own Emotions and Take a Break:** Pause and say something like, "I'm starting to feel overwhelmed, and I want to make sure we can have a productive conversation. I need a few minutes to collect my thoughts. Can we take a short break and come back to this in a little while?" This gives you a chance to regulate your own emotions and prevents further escalation.

2. **Acknowledge the Other Person's Emotions:** As you take a break, you can add a statement that acknowledges their feelings, too. For example, "I can see that you're feeling frustrated/upset/angry as well, and I want to understand where you are coming from." This shows that you're not just focused on your own reactions but also care about their emotional state. It signals that you are taking a timeout to calm down the situation, not to dismiss them.

4. **Practice Self-Regulation:** During the break, use techniques that help you calm down. This could be focusing on your breath to calm your nervous system. You could also take a short walk, splash some water on your face, or listen to calming music.

5. **Encourage Them to Self-Regulate:** Before parting ways for the break, you might gently suggest they also take some time to cool down. For example, you could say, "Maybe you can also take a few deep breaths or do whatever helps you feel calmer, and we'll talk again soon."

Example Conversation:

You: "I'm noticing that I'm starting to feel overwhelmed, and I can see that you're getting frustrated too. I want us to be able to understand each other. I need a few minutes to collect my thoughts. Can we take a 15-minute break and come back to this? Maybe we can both take some deep breaths or do whatever helps us feel calmer during that time."

Partner: "Fine. I'm frustrated because it feels like you're not listening to me."

You: "I understand that you're feeling frustrated, and I really do want to hear what you have to say. Let's take a break, and I promise we'll continue this conversation soon so that I can listen better."

By taking these steps, you're not only managing your own emotions but also helping to de-escalate the situation and create a space for a more productive conversation. You're demonstrating a commitment to resolving the conflict in a healthy and respectful manner. This approach allows both of you to return to the conversation with calmer minds and a greater capacity for empathy and understanding.

Nonviolent Communication (NVC) Technique

Nonviolent Communication (NVC), developed by Marshall Rosenberg, offers a powerful framework for compassionate communication. You can use this to navigate difficult conversations and resolve conflicts peacefully. It's a roadmap to move through disagreements constructively. Remember these four steps: Observation, Feeling, Need, and Request.

Let's walk through a sample dialogue using the NVC method to illustrate its application in a common conflict scenario:

Scenario 1: **Two roommates, Alex and Ben, are having a disagreement about household chores.**

Without NVC:

Alex: "You never do the dishes! The sink is always piled high. You're so inconsiderate."

Ben: "Oh, yeah? Well, you never take out the trash! It's overflowing, and the whole apartment stinks. You're just as bad!"

With NVC:

Alex: "Ben, when I see the sink piled high with dirty dishes (Observation), I feel frustrated (Feeling) because I need our shared living space to be clean (Need). Would you be willing to wash your dishes after each meal (Request)?"

Ben: "I hear you saying that you're frustrated because the sink is full of dishes, and you need our apartment to be clean. Is that right?" (Active Listening, showing empathy)

Alex: "Yes, that's right."

Ben: "Okay. Honestly, when you mentioned it that way, I also felt a little embarrassed (Feeling) because I value being a good roommate (Need). I'm willing to wash my dishes after each meal. And, could I ask you something? When I see the trash overflowing (Observation), I feel a bit overwhelmed (Feeling) because I also need our apartment to be clean (Need). Would you be willing to take out the trash when it's full (Request)?"

Alex: "I understand. I'm willing to do that. Could we sit down together and create a chore schedule that works for both of us (Request)?"

See how different that sounds? By using the NVC framework, Alex and Ben were able to express their needs and feelings without resorting to blame or accusations. They were able to find a solution that worked for both of them, creating a more harmonious living environment.

Scenario 2: **A disagreement with a family member about their constant unsolicited advice.**

Without NVC:

You: "You're always telling me what to do! You never think I can make my own decisions. Just leave me alone!"

Family Member: "I'm just trying to help! You always get so defensive. You should be grateful for my advice."

With NVC:

You: "When I hear unsolicited advice about my decisions (Observation), I feel frustrated and a bit belittled (Feeling) because I need to feel trusted and respected for my ability to make my own choices (Need). Would you be willing to wait for me to ask for your advice before offering it (Request)?"

Family Member: "So, what you are saying is, when I give you advice without you asking for it, you feel like I don't trust your judgment. Is that right?" (Active Listening)

You: "Yes, exactly."

Family Member: "Okay. I understand. When I see you struggling (Observation), I feel worried (Feeling) because I need to know you're okay (Need). But I can see how my advice might come across the wrong way. I'll try to wait until you ask for it."

Scenario 3: Difficult Situation at Work with a Colleague

Problem: A colleague consistently takes credit for your ideas in meetings, leaving you feeling frustrated and unappreciated.

Strategy: Use assertive communication and focus on the behavior, not the person.

"I've noticed that in the past few meetings, the ideas I've contributed have been presented as yours (Observation). I feel undervalued and frustrated when this happens

(Feeling) because I need to be recognized for my contributions (Need). In the future, I'd appreciate it if you could acknowledge my ideas when you present them (Request)."

Observe how NVC can transform a potential argument into a productive conversation. By focusing on observations, feelings, needs, and requests, you create space for understanding and empathy.

These are just some simple examples, of course. But the same principles can be applied to any conflict, big or small.

Forgiveness: The Path to Liberation

Forgiveness plays a crucial role in navigating conflict with grace. It's a powerful tool that can be used in various situations, regardless of the outcome of the conflict. It's not about condoning the other person's behavior or forgetting that it happened; it's about releasing the grip of resentment and anger that can hold you captive, impacting your emotional and mental well-being.

As Nelson Mandela so wisely stated, "Resentment is like drinking poison and then hoping it will kill your enemies."

Resentment is a burden that weighs you down. Forgiveness is about freeing yourself from that pain, allowing yourself to heal and move forward. It is a gift you give yourself, more than anyone else. It's a conscious choice to let go of the negative emotions that are harming you.

The benefits of forgiveness are numerous: reduced stress, improved mental and emotional well-being, and potentially stronger relationships. It allows you to let go of the negative energy that can consume you and create space for more positive emotions, such as compassion, empathy, and peace.

Now, how does forgiveness relate to the Nonviolent Communication (NVC) method we explored earlier? Let's say you've used NVC to address a conflict in a relationship. You've expressed your observations, feelings, needs, and requests, and you've listened empathetically to the other person's perspective.

Scenario 1: The Relationship Improves

If, through using NVC, your relationship has improved, and the other person has shown genuine remorse and a willingness to change their behavior, then forgiveness becomes a natural next step. It allows you to fully release any lingering resentment and move forward with a clean slate. Forgiveness, in this case, strengthens the foundation of the relationship, allowing for deeper trust and intimacy to develop. It becomes a collaborative act, reinforcing the positive changes you've both made.

Scenario 2: The Relationship Does Not Improve

However, what if, despite your best efforts using NVC, the relationship does not improve? What if the other person continues to engage in harmful behavior, violates your boundaries, or refuses to acknowledge your needs? This is where forgiveness becomes a tool for self-liberation.

Forgiveness, in this context, is not about staying in a toxic relationship. There's a difference between forgiving someone and allowing them to continue hurting you. It is, instead, a recognition that you cannot control the other person's actions, but you can control your response. This act of forgiving allows you to detach from the negative emotions associated with the relationship, freeing yourself from the burden of resentment and anger. Ultimately, it is a decision to prioritize your own well-being, even if that means distancing yourself from the other person.

It's vital to recognize when a relationship is consistently causing you harm and not improving despite your efforts. Walking away from a toxic relationship is not a sign of failure; it's an act of self-preservation. It's a courageous decision to prioritize your own mental and emotional health.

Here are some telltale signs that a relationship may be toxic and beyond repair, even with the application of NVC and earnest attempts at forgiveness:

Constant criticism and negativity: The other person consistently puts you down, belittles you, or focuses only on your flaws.

Disrespectful and controlling behavior: They try to control your actions, isolate you from others, or disregard your opinions and feelings.

Emotional or physical abuse: This is never acceptable and a clear sign that you need to remove yourself from the relationship for your own safety.

Consistent violation of your boundaries: Despite clearly communicating your boundaries (as discussed in Chapter 3), the other person continues to disregard them.

A pattern of lying or manipulation: They consistently deceive you, manipulate your emotions, or twist the truth to their advantage.

Feeling drained, anxious, or unhappy after interacting with the person: Your interactions with them consistently leave you feeling depleted, anxious, or emotionally distressed.

If you find yourself in a relationship that consistently exhibits these characteristics, it's crucial to prioritize your well-being. Recall the boundaries we discussed in Chapter 3. This is where they become crucial. Walking away might be the most difficult, but also the most loving thing you can do for yourself. It's an indication of your self-worth and your commitment to your own well-being.

It is important to reiterate that not all people are bad, and forgiveness does not mean you condone bad actions. Forgiveness is a personal journey. Some will be able to reach this point sooner than others. You are the captain of your ship, sailing through life's storms. Sometimes, despite our best efforts, the storm is too strong, and the ship needs to change course. Forgiveness is the compass that aids you navigate those troubled waters, allowing you to release the weight of the past and steer towards a calmer, more peaceful sea. It's about acknowledging that you deserve to be treated with respect and kindness, and that you possess the power to choose relationships that nourish and support your growth.

Navigating conflict with grace is a continuous practice, a dance that requires constant attention, adjustment, and a willingness to learn and grow. There will inevitably be moments when you stumble, lose your footing, or unintentionally step on your partner's toes. That's perfectly acceptable. It's an intrinsic part of the practice that will ultimately lead to mastery of this invaluable skill. Recall the tools you've learned in the previous chapters—self-awareness, compassionate communication, and setting boundaries. These are your trusted partners in this dance, guiding you towards greater harmony and connection. You are now equipped to cultivate relationships that nourish your soul and bring joy to your life. The harmony you seek is within reach, waiting to be discovered.

Key Takeaways

- **Conflict is Inevitable:** Conflict is a natural part of any relationship. How you respond to conflict determines whether it leads to growth or damage.

- **Shift from Ego to Empathy:** Before reacting defensively, pause and try to understand the other person's underlying needs and emotions. This shift in perspective is crucial for dealing with conflict constructively.

- **Master the Art of De-Escalation:** Learn to recognize when a conversation is escalating and use techniques like taking a break and acknowledging both your own and the other person's emotions to calm things down.

- **Use NVC as a Roadmap:** The Nonviolent Communication (NVC) framework—Observation, Feeling, Need, Request—provides a powerful structure for expressing yourself clearly and respectfully, even during difficult conversations.

- **Forgiveness is Freedom:** Forgiveness, whether the relationship improves or not, is a powerful tool for freeing yourself from the weight of resentment and anger. It's about prioritizing your own well-being. Sometimes, forgiveness means walking away, and that's okay.

∼

Chapter 5

THE SINGULARITY

A true lover is proved such by his pain of hear,

No sickness is there like sickness of heart.

The lover's ailment is different from all ailments;

Love is the astrolabe of God's mysteries.

However much we describe and explain love,

When we fall in love we are ashamed of our words.

Explanation by the tongue makes most things clear,

But love unexplained is clearer.

– Rumi

In these evocative verses, Rumi deciphers the astounding and often paradoxical nature of love, a feeling that lies at the very heart of intimacy. He speaks of the "pain of heart," the "sickness of heart" that accompanies true love, intimating that vulnerability and a willingness to perceive the full spectrum of human emotion are essential elements of deep connection. Rumi calls love "the astrolabe of God's mysteries," implying that it is through love that we glimpse the divine, that we touch the deepest truths about ourselves and the universe.

He acknowledges the limitations of language in describing the experience of love, hinting at the inadequacy of words to capture its depth and complexity. And yet, paradoxically, Rumi suggests that "love unexplained is clearer." He writes, "When we fall in love we are ashamed of our words." This shame stems not just from the inadequacy of language, but also from a sense that our words might cheapen or misrepresent the intense, personal, and almost sacred experience of love. It's as if articulating it with clumsy words diminishes its sheer beauty. This points to the intuitive, nonverbal nature of intimacy, the unspoken understanding that exists between two deeply connected souls, a connection that transcends the realm of words.

The Journey to Oneness

There's an interesting story that beautifully illustrates this concept in Rumi's Masnavi. Let's explore it:

A man who was deeply in love went to his beloved's house and knocked excitedly on the door. "Who's there?" she asked. "It's me," he replied, full of hope. But she said, "Go away, there's no room for you here! You're not ready yet. You say 'It's me' and still claim to love me? A true lover doesn't just see himself." She wouldn't open the door, and the heartbroken man eventually left.

He went away to a faraway place, suffering from the pain of being apart from her. After a year, he returned and went to her house again. This time, he knocked very gently. "Who's knocking?" she asked impatiently. "No one! It's you on this side of the door too," he answered humbly.

"Now that you've stopped thinking only about yourself, you've finally become me! Two separate people can't exist in this house, but now you may come in," she said. She opened the door and let him in. "You're welcome here now. There's no difference between us anymore. We're not like the rose and the thorn, separate and distinct. We are one."

Essentially, the story illustrates that true love isn't selfish. At first, the man was only thinking about himself and his own desires. He had to go through a period of hardship and self-reflection before he could understand that real love means seeing yourself as one with the person you love. Only then was he ready to be with his beloved. They had to be on the same page, sharing the same spirit, otherwise, their relationship would have been meaningless.

This story provides a rich analogy for the multifaceted nature of intimacy. It highlights that true intimacy is a path that requires self-awareness, humility, personal growth, and a move away from self-centeredness to oneness with the other. The story portrays intimacy as more than just a feeling, but as a union of two souls where individual boundaries blur and merge. This emphasizes that intimacy is not simply physical closeness, but a deep, transformative experience that changes both individuals.

This chapter is about exploring the same multifaceted nature of intimacy, moving beyond the limitations of words to champion the unspoken language of the heart, a language of vulnerability, empathy, and trust. We will be weaving a tapestry of connection that is both astounding and enduring, reflecting the "mysteries" that Rumi alludes to, creating a bond that goes beyond what words can express.

Exploring Different Dimensions of Intimacy

Intimacy is often misunderstood as being solely about physical closeness or romantic love. But it's so much more than that. **True intimacy encompasses a range**

of connections that nourish our souls. Let's explore different types of intimacy:

- **Emotional Intimacy:** This is the ability to share your feelings openly and honestly with another person, without fear of judgment or rejection. It's about being vulnerable and authentic, allowing yourself to be seen for who you truly are.

- **Intellectual Intimacy:** This involves connecting with someone on a mental level, sharing ideas, thoughts, and perspectives. It is fostered by engaging in stimulating conversations, challenging each other's minds, and growing together intellectually. For example, you might spend hours discussing different philosophical concepts, engaging in a passionate debate, or working together on a creative project.

- **Spiritual Intimacy:** This is a connection that transcends the physical and mental spheres. It can involve sharing a common faith or spiritual practice, or simply a deep sense of connection to something larger than yourselves.

- **Physical Intimacy:** This includes physical touch, affection, and sexual connection. While it's often associated with romantic relationships, physical intimacy can also be expressed through platonic touch, such as a hug from a friend or a comforting hand on the shoulder.

It's important to note that these types of intimacy are not mutually exclusive. They often overlap and intertwine, creating a rich tapestry of connection in our relationships. You can experience all of them in a romantic partnership, and different types with friends and family.

Barriers to Intimacy

We all crave connection, but sometimes getting close to others can feel scary. We seem to have these invisible walls built around us. These walls are natural defenses, built from past experiences and our own self-doubt. Here are a few of the most common ones:

- **Fear of Rejection:** This is a big one. We're wired to want to belong, so the thought of being rejected can be terrifying. It's like our inner child is afraid of being left out in the cold. This fear can make us hesitant to open up and show our true selves. We worry, what if they don't like what they see?

- **Past Hurts:** Been burned before? It's natural to want to protect yourself. Past betrayals or disappointments can make us wary of trusting again. We might think, "If I let someone in, they'll just hurt me like the last time."

- **Attachment Baggage:** Think back to our discussion about attachment styles in Chapter 1. Our early childhood experiences shape how we relate to others. If we didn't have a secure base growing up, it can be tough to form close bonds later in life. We might be clingy and anxious, or we might push people away— all because of those early blueprints.

- **Low Self-Esteem:** If we don't feel good about ourselves, it's hard to believe that anyone else will. It's like we have a little voice inside that says, "You're not good enough." This can make us sabotage relationships or settle for less than we deserve, fearing that we are unworthy of true love and acceptance.

These barriers are like our own personal security systems—designed to protect us, but sometimes they end up keeping out the very things we crave. The good news is, with a little courage and self-awareness, we can start to lower those walls and let love in. And this requires us to be brave, to challenge those inner fears, and to learn to trust again, both ourselves and others. Have patience as it is a gradual process, and it's perfectly acceptable to seek support along the way.

Cultivating Vulnerability

As Brené Brown stated, "Vulnerability is the birthplace of love, belonging, joy, courage, empathy, and creativity." It is the key that unlocks the door to deeper connections and more meaningful relationships. It is in those moments of vulnerability that we allow ourselves to be truly seen and known.

Vulnerability is the gateway to intimacy. But it's not enough to simply say, "Let your guard down." Here are some actionable steps to help you become more vulnerable:

- **Start Small:** Share a personal story or express an emotion you usually keep to yourself with someone you trust. It could be as simple as admitting you're feeling nervous about a presentation or sharing a childhood memory.

- **Practice Self-Compassion:** As we learned in our discussion on boundaries, self-love is crucial. Treat yourself with the same kindness and understanding that you would offer a friend. This will make it easier to be vulnerable with others.

- **Use "I" Statements:** Summon up the power of "I" statements from Chapter 2. They are invaluable here, too. Expressing your feelings using "I" statements allows you to be vulnerable without blaming or accusing others.

- **Accept Imperfection:** Recognize that vulnerability is not about being perfect. It's about being real. It's okay to show your flaws and insecurities. In fact, that's often where the deepest connections are made.

Responding to Vulnerability with Empathy and Grace

When someone chooses to be vulnerable with you, it's a precious gift. It's an invitation into their inner world, a sign of trust and a desire for deeper connection. How you respond in those moments can either strengthen the bond of intimacy or create distance. As we explored in

Chapter 2, empathy is the cornerstone of connection. It's the ability to understand and share the feelings of another person. When someone is vulnerable, they're often sharing emotions that are raw and sensitive.

The Quran beautifully underscores the importance of this empathetic connection, particularly within intimate relationships. In Surah Ar-Rum, it states:

"And one of His signs is that He created for you spouses from among yourselves so that you may find comfort in them. And He has placed between you compassion and mercy. Surely in this are signs for people who reflect."

(Surah Ar-Rum, 30:21)

This verse highlights the divine intention behind intimate relationships—to be a source of tranquility, affection, and mercy. It reminds us that these relationships are meant to be havens, places where we can find solace and support during the storms of life. The "compassion and mercy" mentioned here are not passive feelings but active responses, mirroring the empathy we discussed earlier. They call upon us to meet vulnerability with realization and kindness, and to offer comfort and support when our loved ones are hurting. It is within this compassionate space that true intimacy can blossom.

Further emphasizing the interconnectedness within intimate partnerships, the Quran states in Surah Al-Baqarah:

**"Your spouses are a garment for you as
you are for them."**

(Surah Al-Baqarah, 2:187)

This "garment" metaphor is incredibly powerful. Think about what a garment does: it provides protection, warmth, and comfort. It conceals our vulnerabilities and presents a certain image to the world. In the context of a relationship, this verse suggests that partners provide a similar kind of emotional and spiritual covering for each other. Just as a garment shields us from the elements, our partners offer us a safe space where we can be our authentic selves, where our vulnerabilities are protected, and where we can find comfort and support.

It implies a reciprocal relationship of mutual protection and care. You are their safe harbor, as they are for you. The "garment" also represents a closeness and intimacy that is unique to this type of bond. Just as a garment is close to the skin, our partners are close to our hearts, sharing our innermost thoughts and feelings.

Therefore, when someone chooses to be vulnerable with you, they are, in essence, removing a layer of themselves, entrusting you with their inner self. Responding with empathy, compassion, and mercy is not just a kind act, but a sacred responsibility. This means honoring the trust they've placed in you and reciprocating by providing a safe and supportive space for their vulnerability. By doing so, we strengthen the fabric of intimacy, creating a relationship where both partners can find solace, strength, and a sense of belonging.

Here are some ways to practice empathy:

Pay attention not only to their words but also to their body language and tone of voice. After they've finished speaking, reflect back their feelings using phrases like, "It sounds like you're feeling overwhelmed because..." or "I hear that you're heartbroken about..." This shows that you're truly listening and making an effort to understand their perspective. Follow this up by validating their emotions. Let them know that their feelings are understandable and acceptable. You can say, "It makes perfect sense that you'd feel that way," or "That sounds incredibly difficult; your feelings are valid."

Building a Foundation of Intimacy with Trust

Responding to vulnerability with empathy and grace is a crucial part of building trust. And be mindful that trust is not built overnight; it takes time, like constructing a sturdy building brick by brick. It requires consistent effort and a commitment to acting in trustworthy ways.

Here are some practical steps you can take to foster trust, particularly when someone is entrusting you with their vulnerability:

- **Keep Their Confidence:** When someone shares something personal with you, honor their trust by keeping it confidential. Unless they've given you explicit permission, don't share their story with others. This demonstrates that you are a safe and reliable person to confide in.

- **Be Non-Judgmental:** As we explored earlier, create a safe space where they feel comfortable sharing without fear of judgment. This will encourage them to open up further in the future.

- **Be Present and Attentive:** Give them your undivided attention. Put away distractions, make eye contact, and truly listen to what they're saying. This shows that you value them and their feelings.

- **Keep Your Commitments:** If you say you'll do something, do it. This demonstrates your reliability and shows that you value your word, not just when things are easy, but when it counts.

- **Be Honest and Transparent:** Open and honest communication, as we learned in Chapter 2, is essential for building trust. Share your thoughts and feelings honestly, even if it seems difficult, and encourage them to do the same.

- **Show Respect:** Treat others with kindness, consideration, and respect, even when you disagree with them. Recall the boundaries we discussed in Chapter 3—respecting others' boundaries is crucial for building trust.

- **Be Consistent:** Trust is built through consistent actions over time. Small, everyday acts of trustworthiness create a foundation of trust that can weather difficult times.

- **Admit Mistakes:** We all make mistakes. When you do, own up to it, apologize sincerely, and make amends if possible. This shows that you're willing to take responsibility for your actions and that you value the relationship.

Assessing and Navigating Intimacy Levels

How do you know if there's genuine intimacy in a relationship? Intimacy is characterized by a sense of closeness, trust, and mutual understanding. It's a feeling of being safe and accepted. You feel comfortable being vulnerable, sharing your thoughts and feelings, and knowing that the other person will respond with empathy and respect. It's an experience of being truly seen, accepted, and loved for who you are, including your flaws and mistakes.

Here are some key indicators that signify the presence of intimacy in a relationship:

1. Open and Honest Communication: This forms the bedrock of any intimate relationship. You feel comfortable talking about anything, even difficult topics, without fear of judgment or reprisal. It's not just about sharing the good things; it's also about being able to express your fears, insecurities, and vulnerabilities.

- You can share both positive and negative emotions without feeling like you have to censor yourself. You don't have to put on a brave face or pretend everything is okay when it's not.

- You can disagree without shutting down or attacking each other. You can navigate conflict constructively, using the skills we discussed in Chapter 4, knowing that your differences won't damage the underlying connection.

- You can talk about your hopes, dreams, and aspirations, as well as your fears and disappointments. You feel safe sharing your inner world with the other person, knowing they will listen with empathy and understanding.

- There's a sense of transparency and authenticity in your communication. You're not afraid to be real with each other, even if it seems uncomfortable.

2. Mutual Respect and Admiration: In an intimate relationship, you value and appreciate each other's qualities, perspectives, and differences. It's not about putting the other person on a pedestal, but about genuinely admiring their strengths and accepting their weaknesses.

- You appreciate each other's unique talents and abilities. You celebrate each other's successes and offer support during challenges.

• You respect each other's opinions and values, even when they differ from your own. You don't try to change the other person or force them to conform to your beliefs.

• You admire each other's character and integrity. You see the good in each other, even when you're facing difficulties.

• You treat each other with kindness, consideration, and respect, both in public and in private. You speak highly of each other to others and avoid gossiping or complaining about your partner behind their back.

3. Emotional Safety: This is the feeling of being able to express your emotions without fear of judgment, rejection, or ridicule. It's about trusting that the other person will respond with empathy and kindness, even when you're struggling emotionally.

• You feel safe to cry, laugh, express anger, or show any other emotion without feeling like you'll be judged or dismissed. You know that your feelings will be validated, even if the other person doesn't necessarily share them.

• You can be vulnerable without feeling like you need to put up walls or defenses. You trust that the other person will handle your vulnerability with care.

• You don't have to walk on eggshells around each other. You can be yourself, without fear of triggering a negative reaction.

- You feel accepted for who you are. You don't feel like you have to hide parts of yourself to be loved.

4. Shared Vulnerability: Both of you are willing to be open and vulnerable with each other. This involves sharing your fears, insecurities, and past experiences, even the ones that are painful or embarrassing. This means letting your guard down and allowing the other person to see the real you.

- You're willing to take emotional risks, knowing that there's a chance you might get hurt. But you also trust that the potential rewards of deeper connection outweigh the risks.

- You share your inner world with each other—your hopes, dreams, fears, and disappointments. You don't just talk about surface-level topics; you dig into the deeper aspects of your being.

- You're willing to admit your mistakes and apologize when you're wrong. You don't let pride or ego get in the way of repairing the relationship.

- You're able to ask for help when you need it, knowing that the other person will be there for you. You don't feel like you have to be strong and independent all the time.

5. Deep Understanding: In an intimate relationship, you feel truly seen and understood by the other person. They get you, even when you don't fully understand yourself. It's a feeling of being deeply known and accepted.

- They understand your quirks, your triggers, and your love language. They know what makes you tick, both good and bad.

- They can often anticipate your needs and feelings, even before you express them. It's as if they have an intuitive sense of what's going on inside you.

- They see your potential, even when you doubt yourself. They believe in you, even when you're struggling to believe in yourself.

- You feel a sense of deep connection as if you're on the same wavelength. You can often communicate without words, simply by a look or a touch.

These hallmarks of intimacy create a powerful bond between two individuals, a bond that can weather the storms of life and provide a source of strength, comfort, and joy. But it requires ongoing effort and nurturing. Working on these things in your relationships will make your relationships richer and more meaningful.

Addressing a Lack of Intimacy

What if intimacy is lacking?

If you feel intimacy is lacking in a relationship, it's fundamental to first reflect on your contributions. Are you creating a safe space for vulnerability? Are you practicing active listening and empathy? Are you being trustworthy and consistent in your actions?

If you're doing your part and intimacy is still lacking, it might be time to have an open and honest conversation with the other person. Using the "I" statements we discussed in Chapter 2, express your desire for a deeper connection. For example, you could say, "I've been feeling a bit distant from you lately, and I value our connection. I'd like us to be able to share more openly with each other. What are your thoughts on this?"

It's important to be mindful of the fact that not everyone is comfortable with the same level of intimacy. Some people may have had past experiences that make it difficult for them to open up. Others may simply have different needs and preferences when it comes to closeness. It's crucial to respect the other person's boundaries and not try to force them to be more intimate than they're comfortable with.

Prophet Muhammad (peace be upon him) said, "Allah is Kind and loves kindness, and He rewards for kindness in a way that He does not reward for harshness." (Musnad Ahmad 902)

This Hadith encourages us to approach our relationships with gentleness and compassion. Kindness is a key ingredient in building strong and lasting connections. And sometimes, kindness means accepting that a relationship may not reach the level of intimacy we desire, and that's okay. This means finding peace with where the relationship is, and appreciating the connection for what it is, rather than what we wish it could be.

Integrating Intimacy into Daily Life

Intimacy isn't just reserved for special occasions. It can be woven into the fabric of our everyday lives. Here are some ideas for cultivating intimacy in your daily interactions:

- **Create Shared Rituals:** Establish daily or weekly rituals that foster connection, such as having dinner together without distractions, taking a walk together after work, or having a weekly phone call with a long-distance friend.

- **Practice Gratitude:** Express your appreciation for the people in your life, both verbally and through small gestures. A simple "thank you" or a thoughtful act of kindness can go a long way.

- **Engage in Meaningful Conversations:** Go beyond surface-level small talk. Ask open-ended questions that encourage deeper sharing, such as, "What was the highlight of your day?" or "What are you most grateful for right now?"

- **Offer Thoughtful Gestures:** Small acts of kindness and consideration can speak volumes. This could be anything from making someone a cup of tea to offering to help with a chore to sending a heartfelt text message.

- **Be Present:** When you're with someone, give them your full attention. Put away your phone, make eye contact, and truly listen to what they have to say.

Recall the lessons from previous chapters: self-awareness, compassionate communication, healthy boundaries, and navigating conflict with grace. These are the threads that, when woven together, create an astounding tapestry of intimacy. You are now ready to experience the fullness of human connection, to experience the joy of belonging, and to create a life that is rich in love, meaning, and purpose. Let us continue this journey together, weaving a world where love and empathy prevail.

Key Takeaways

- **Intimacy Goes Beyond Words:** True intimacy involves a deep, often unspoken connection that transcends language. It's an experience of feeling seen, understood, and accepted for who you truly are.

- **Vulnerability is the Key:** Opening yourself up to vulnerability, even with the risk of pain, is essential for building genuine intimacy. It requires courage and a willingness to share your authentic self.

- **Trust is Built Brick by Brick:** Trust, the foundation of intimacy, is built gradually through consistent actions, honesty, and respecting boundaries. It's about being reliable and honoring the confidence shared with you.

- **Empathy Fuels Connection:** Responding to another's vulnerability with empathy and compassion strengthens the bond of intimacy. It involves actively listening, validating their feelings, and offering support.

- **Intimacy Requires Nurturing:** Weaving intimacy into daily life through shared rituals, meaningful conversations, and acts of kindness keeps the connection vibrant and strong.

~

Chapter 6

THE CIRCLE OF BELONGING

No lover ever seeks union with his beloved,

But his beloved is also seeking union with him.

The noise of clapping of hands is never heard

From one of thy hands unaided by the other hand

The man athirst cries, "Where is delicious water?"

Water too cries, "Where is the water-drinker?"

This thirst in my soul is the attraction of the water;

I am the water's and the water is mine.

God's wisdom in His eternal foreknowledge and decree

Made us to be lovers one of the other.

Nay more, all the parts of the world by this decree

Are arranged in pairs, and each loves its mate.

Every part of the world desires its mate,

Just as amber attracts blades of straw.

– Rumi

These lines from Rumi speak to the fundamental human need for connection, a reciprocal yearning that lies at the heart of belonging. Just as the lover seeks the beloved, and the beloved seeks the lover. We, too, are driven by an innate desire to connect with others, to form bonds of community and support. Rumi's verses remind us that this desire for connection is not a one-way street; it's a mutual longing, a shared human experience. The imagery of two hands clapping, the thirsty man and the water seeking each other, and amber attracting straw all point to the interconnectedness of all things. We are not isolated beings, but rather parts of a larger whole, drawn to each other like magnets.

This chapter is about exploring the power of that connection, the "circle of belonging" that sustains us, nourishes us, and empowers us to make a difference in the world. We will discover that the need for community is a fundamental aspect of our humanity, not a weakness. By building strong, supportive communities, we both enrich our own lives and contribute to the well-being of the world. This journey leads us to the realization that we are all interconnected, our personal paths interwoven with those of others.

The Fundamental Need for Connection

We, at our core, are social beings—intrinsically wired for connection. From the very moment we draw our first breath, we seek out relationships with others. We crave belonging, acceptance, and a sense of community. It's embedded in our very DNA. This isn't just a "nice-to-have"—it's a fundamental need. Just like we need food, water, and shelter to survive, we need good connections to thrive. Our brains are physiologically wired to connect with others, and when this fundamental need is unmet, we suffer both mentally and emotionally.

The Quran powerfully emphasizes the paramount importance of unity and brotherhood, stating:

"And hold firmly to the rope of Allah all together and do not become divided. And remember the favor of Allah upon you - when you were enemies and He brought your hearts together and you became, by His favor, brothers."

(Surah Ali 'Imran, 3:103)

This verse highlights the strength and blessings that come from unity and connection. It's a reminder that we are stronger together, that our shared humanity is a source of resilience and support. It also emphasizes that division and discord weaken the community, while unity and mutual support strengthen it. By holding firmly to shared values and working together, communities can overcome challenges and achieve great things. This is not just about avoiding conflict, but about actively cultivating relationships built on trust, respect, and love. It is a call to action, urging us to be proactive in building bridges and fostering understanding within our communities.

The Illusion of Connection in the Digital Age

The digital age revolution makes it harder to define genuine human connection, often making us think online interactions are enough. We might have hundreds or even thousands of "friends" on social media, but how many of those connections are truly meaningful? How many of those people truly know us, and how many do we truly know? While technology can be a useful tool for staying in touch and maintaining existing relationships, it can also create a false sense of connection that leaves us feeling more isolated than ever. Scrolling through curated feeds of other people's seemingly perfect lives can trigger feelings of envy and inadequacy, further eroding our sense of belonging. The likes, comments, and shares can become a substitute for genuine interaction, leaving us craving real human contact.

While online platforms can provide a sense of community for some, they often lack the depth and authenticity of face-to-face interactions. This is not to say that all online interaction is bad. Technology can be a great way to stay connected with loved ones who live far away, or to find communities of people who share our interests. However, it's necessary to be mindful of how we're using technology and to make sure that it's enhancing, rather than detracting from, our real-life relationships. It is about finding a healthy balance.

The bottom line is that online connections, while convenient and sometimes necessary, cannot fully replace the fundamental human need for real, in-person belonging. Belonging is more than just feeling included or accepted; it's the feeling of being seen, heard, and valued for who you truly are. It's about finding your people, the ones who get you, who understand you, who accept you. It means knowing that you're not alone, that there are others who share your values, your interests, and your experiences. It's about forming relationships where you can be your authentic self, without the pressure to present a curated or idealized version of yourself. This is the kind of belonging that nourishes our souls and allows us to thrive.

Finding Your Tribe

So how do we find our tribe? Here are some practical tips:

1. Identify Your Passions: Ask yourself: What are you truly passionate about? What activities make you lose track of time? Joining groups or clubs related to your interests is a great way to meet like-minded people.

- If you love reading, join a book club at your local library or bookstore. You'll instantly have something in common with the other members, and you can engage in stimulating conversations about your favorite authors and genres.

- If you're passionate about fitness, sign up for a group fitness class like Yoga, Zumba, or Crossfit. You'll meet people who share your interest in health and wellness, and you can encourage each other on your fitness goals.

- If you're a creative person, consider taking a painting, pottery, or writing class. You'll be surrounded by people who share your artistic inclinations, and you can learn from each other and inspire each other's creativity.

2. Be Proactive: Don't wait for others to approach you. Take the initiative to introduce yourself, start conversations, and invite people to do things. Everyone is looking for a valuable connection, and most people will appreciate your efforts.

- At a social gathering, instead of sticking with the people you already know, make an effort to introduce yourself to someone new. A simple "Hi, I'm [your name]. How do you know the host?" can be a great conversation starter.

- If you hit it off with someone in a class or group, don't be afraid to suggest grabbing coffee or lunch sometime. You could say something like, "I've really enjoyed our conversations. Would you be interested in getting together outside of class sometime?"

- If you hear about an event that you think a new acquaintance might enjoy, invite them to join you. You could say, "I'm going to this concert next weekend. I think you'd really like it. Want to come along?"

3. Challenge Yourself: When you join a group, challenge yourself to connect with at least two new people during each meeting. This will help you expand your circle and build connections more quickly.

- Before attending a group meeting, set a goal to introduce yourself to at least two people you haven't met before. Prepare a few open-ended questions to ask them, such as "What brought you to this group?" or "What are you working on these days?"

- During a group activity, make an effort to partner with someone you don't know well. This will give you a chance to interact with them in a more focused setting and learn more about their interests.

- After a meeting, approach someone you found interesting and strike up a conversation. You could say something like, "I really enjoyed what you said about [topic]. I'd love to hear more about your perspective."

4. Volunteer Your Time: Giving back to your community is a powerful way to connect with others who share your values. Find a cause you care about and get involved. You'll meet people who are passionate about making a difference, and you'll feel good about contributing to something meaningful.

- If you're passionate about animals, volunteer at a local animal shelter. You'll meet other animal lovers, and you'll make a difference in the lives of animals in need.

• If you care about environmental issues, volunteer for a park cleanup or a community garden project. You'll connect with people who share your concern for the environment, and you'll contribute to making your community a better place.

• If you're interested in helping children, volunteer as a tutor or mentor at a local school or community center. You'll meet other people who are passionate about education, and you'll make a positive impact on the lives of young people.

5. Reconnect with Old Friends: Life gets busy, and it's easy to lose touch with people. Reach out to old friends and see if you can rekindle those connections. You might be surprised at how much you still have in common, and it can be incredibly rewarding to reconnect with someone from your past.

• Send a text or email to a friend you haven't seen in a while, proposing a get-together for coffee or lunch. You could say something like, "Hey! It's been too long. How are you doing? I'd love to catch up sometime soon."

• Look up old friends on social media and send them a message. You could say something like, "I came across your profile the other day, and it made me think of all the fun times we used to have. How have you been?"

• If you hear about a major life event happening for an old friend, such as a wedding or the birth of a child, reach out and offer your congratulations. This can be a great way to re-establish contact and rekindle the friendship.

6. Be Open to New Experiences: Step outside of your comfort zone and try something new. You never know who you might meet or what new interests you might discover. This can open up a whole new world of possibilities for connection.

• Sign up for a class or workshop on a topic that interests you, even if you don't know anyone else who's taking it. You might discover a new passion and meet people who share your curiosity.

• Attend a local event or festival that you wouldn't normally go to. This could be a concert, a play, a food festival, or anything else that piques your interest.

• Travel to a new place, even if it's just for a weekend getaway. This can expose you to new cultures, new perspectives, and new people.

Building and maintaining strong relationships takes effort and intention. It's like tending a garden. You need to water the plants, pull the weeds, and provide the right conditions for growth, but the rewards are immeasurable. By actively seeking out opportunities to connect with others, you'll be well on your way to building a supportive and fulfilling community.

Nurturing Your Tribe: Building a Strong and Supportive Community

Finding your tribe is a momentous step, but it's just the beginning of building a truly supportive and thriving community. A community needs consistent engagement to nurture the relationships of its members. It involves transforming those initial connections into lasting bonds of mutual support, shared purpose, and collective growth.

The Quran emphasizes the importance of collective responsibility and mutual support within a community, stating:

> **"Let there be a group among you who call 'others' to goodness, encourage what is good, and forbid what is evil—it is they who will be successful."**

> **(Surah Ali 'Imran, 3:104)**

This verse highlights the significance of actively promoting good and discouraging harmful actions within a community. It suggests that a collective effort towards righteousness is essential for the success and well-being of the whole group. This emphasizes the power of a community to shape the behavior of its members and to create a positive environment. By encouraging good deeds and discouraging harmful ones, the community creates a culture of virtue and mutual support. This can involve actively promoting ethical behavior, intervening in situations where harm is being done, and providing guidance and support to those who are struggling. The verse also highlights the importance of leadership within a community, suggesting that there should be individuals who take responsibility for guiding the group toward righteousness.

Prophet Muhammad (peace be upon him) said, "A believer to another believer is like a building whose different parts enforce each other." (Sahih al-Bukhari 481)

This hadith emphasizes that just as the various parts of a building rely on each other for stability and strength, so do the members of a community rely on each other for support and well-being. It highlights the importance of unity, cooperation, and mutual reliance within a community. Every member of the community, regardless of their individual strengths or weaknesses, has something valuable to contribute. By working together and supporting each other, the community becomes stronger and more resilient. This analogy encourages us to view ourselves as integral parts of a larger whole, working together towards a common goal.

Let's draw valuable lessons from an allegorical tale found in Rumi's Masnavi:

A tired merchant arrived at a resting place for travelers late in the day. He took the load off his camel but didn't tie it up properly. The rope came loose, and the camel started to wander off. A little mouse saw the rope trailing on the ground, grabbed it in her mouth, and ran in front of the camel. The camel, being bored, thought it was funny and let the mouse lead him along.

The mouse started to feel really proud of herself, thinking she was some kind of hero for leading such a big animal. The camel noticed the mouse getting all puffed up with pride but pretended not to. He figured he'd let her enjoy her moment of glory.

They walked for a while until they came to a wide stream. To the mouse, it looked like a huge, endless river. She climbed up a little hill to try to see the other side, but it was too far away. The camel knew why the mouse had stopped but acted like he didn't. "Hey, why did you stop? Let's go!" he said, kind of teasing her.

"The water is too deep and fast! I'm scared I'll drown," the mouse cried out. "Let me check," said the camel, stepping into the water. "You're being silly; it's not deep at all! It only comes up to my knees." "Well, to you it might seem like nothing, but to me, it's like a huge obstacle! We're not the same size, you know," the mouse pleaded.

"Maybe you shouldn't have been so bold, trying to lead a camel when you should have stuck with someone your own size," the camel pointed out. "I'm sorry, I'm sorry," the mouse said sincerely. "Help me cross, and I'll never let my pride get the better of me again."

The camel felt sorry for the little mouse. "Climb up on my hump," he said kindly. "Crossing this is easy for me. I could carry hundreds of you at once!" And so, the camel and the mouse continued on together, helping each other out from then on.

The story teaches us about the dangers of pride and the importance of knowing your limitations. The mouse got carried away with her own sense of importance, but she learned a valuable lesson when she faced a challenge she couldn't handle on her own. It also shows that even those who are very different can help each other out and form a strong bond by working together.

This situation paints a picture of the social and economic divides that can exist within a community, showing us how pride can prevent people from coming together. It reminds us that within any community, there are vulnerable individuals who depend on the support of others, and it's our collective responsibility to see and address those needs. To build a truly supportive community, we must cultivate empathy and compassion, translating those feelings into tangible acts of assistance. When we offer support, we create a mutually beneficial relationship, where everyone's strengths are utilized for the betterment of the whole. A truly supportive community recognizes the inherent value of each member, actively addresses vulnerabilities, and fosters a culture of giving and receiving. This is how a group of individuals transforms into a unified whole, bound by the threads of genuine connection.

As Margaret Mead famously said, "Never doubt that a small group of thoughtful, committed citizens can change the world; indeed, it's the only thing that ever has." This quote highlights the power of the community to create positive change, starting with a small group and expanding outward.

The Quran further emphasizes the interconnectedness and mutual responsibility within a community:

"The believers, both men and women, are guardians of one another. They encourage good and forbid evil,"

(Surah At-Tawbah, 9:71)

This verse highlights the importance of mutual support and guidance among believers, suggesting that community members are responsible for looking out for each other's well-being, both spiritually and materially. This involves actively promoting positive behaviors and discouraging harmful ones, creating a culture of accountability and mutual care. The phrase "guardians of one another" implies a deep level of interconnectedness, where the actions of one individual impact the others. It's about recognizing that we are all in this together and that our well-being is intertwined with the well-being of those around us.

Here's a roadmap for cultivating a strong and lively community once you've found your people:

1. Foster a Culture of Reciprocity and Support:

A strong community is built on a foundation of mutual support and reciprocity. Encourage a culture where members actively look for ways to help and uplift each other. This could involve offering practical assistance, lending a listening ear, sharing resources, or simply celebrating each other's successes. It's not about keeping score, but about creating a virtuous cycle where giving and receiving become natural parts of the community dynamic.

2. Create Opportunities for Shared Experiences:

Shared experiences are the glue that holds a community together. Organize regular gatherings, events, or activities that allow members to connect on a deeper level. This could be anything from potlucks and game nights to workshops and outings. The key is to create opportunities for meaningful interaction and shared memories that strengthen bonds between members and create a sense of collective identity.

3. Adopt Service and Collective Action:

As mentioned earlier, service to others is a powerful way to foster a sense of belonging and purpose. Encourage your community to engage in acts of service, both within the group and in the wider world. This could involve volunteering for a local cause, supporting a member in need, or working together on a project that benefits the community as a whole. Each individual plays a vital role in supporting and uplifting the others. It's a reminder that we are all interconnected, and by working together towards a shared purpose, you not only strengthen your bonds but also amplify your collective impact.

4. Cultivate Open and Honest Communication:

Just as in personal relationships, open and honest communication is essential for a thriving community. Encourage members to share their thoughts, feelings, and needs openly and respectfully. Create a safe space where people feel comfortable expressing themselves without fear of judgment or reprisal. This includes actively listening to each other, using the techniques we explored in previous chapters, and creating channels for feedback and constructive dialogue.

5. Practice Vulnerability and Authenticity:

Vulnerability, as we explored in Chapter 5, is essential for building deep connections. Encourage members to share their authentic selves, including their struggles and imperfections. Create a culture where vulnerability is seen as a strength, not a weakness. When people feel safe to be themselves, it creates a sense of trust and intimacy that strengthens the community as a whole.

6. Establish Shared Values and Purpose:

While your tribe may have formed around shared interests, it's vital to establish a deeper sense of shared values and purpose. What are the core principles that guide your community? What is your collective vision for the future? Having a shared understanding of your values and purpose will help you navigate challenges, make decisions, and stay aligned as you grow.

7. Navigate Conflict with Grace:

Conflict is inevitable in any group setting. As we learned in Chapter 4, disagreements, when handled constructively, can strengthen relationships. Encourage members to approach conflict as an opportunity for growth and understanding, using the tools of compassionate communication and empathy. Establish clear guidelines for conflict resolution and create a culture where disagreements are addressed with respect and a willingness to find common ground.

8. Celebrate Diversity and Inclusivity:

A thriving community welcomes diversity in all its forms. Encourage members to appreciate and respect each other's differences, whether they be in background, perspective, or experience. Create a welcoming and inclusive environment where everyone feels valued and respected for who they are. This diversity of thought and experience will enrich the community and foster creativity and innovation.

9. Connect to the Wider World:

Encourage your community to engage with the wider world, to make a positive impact beyond your immediate circle. Working together towards a shared goal allows us to achieve results far beyond what we could accomplish individually. We can make a real difference in the world, extending the positive ripple effect of our strong community outwards.

By implementing these strategies, you can transform your tribe into a thriving community that provides support, belonging, and purpose. By constant effort and unrelenting commitment, you'll not only enrich your own life but also contribute to creating a more connected and compassionate world.

Key Takeaways

- **Belonging is a Fundamental Need:** We are wired for connection. Feeling a sense of belonging is as essential to our well-being as food and water. Online connections alone are not enough to fulfill this need.

- **Actively Seek Your Tribe:** Finding your tribe—people who share your values and interests—requires proactive effort. Identify your passions, join groups, volunteer, and be open to new experiences.

- **Nurture Your Relationships:** Building a strong community requires consistent effort. Create opportunities for shared experiences, foster open communication, and encourage a culture of mutual support.

- **Honor Service and Vulnerability:** Serving others and being willing to be vulnerable within your community deepens connections and fosters a sense of purpose.

- **Community Creates Change:** A strong, supportive community not only enriches the lives of its members but also has the power to make a positive impact on the wider world. By working together, you can achieve far more than you ever could alone.

And so, we come full circle, back to the heart of it all: connection. Throughout this journey, we've explored deeply the concepts of self-awareness, compassionate communication, healthy boundaries, navigating conflict, and cultivating intimacy. These are not just concepts, but tools—powerful instruments that, when wielded with intention and care, can help you build a thriving community. Bear in mind, it all begins with the willingness to look within, to understand your own patterns, and to practice vulnerability. The world is waiting for the unique contribution that only you can make, the light that shines from your own beautifully polished mirror. Value your circle of belonging, step into the fullness of your potential, and together, let us create a world where every individual feels seen, heard, valued, and deeply connected—a world where love, compassion, and kindness prevail.

···•··•··•··~···

Let Love Be Your Guide

Let's end this book with a promise, a shared promise between you and me, to carry the lessons we've learned into the world, building bridges of empathy and kindness. You have what it takes; I have faith in you. You've explored the intricate reality of human connection, guided by the poetic wisdom of Rumi, the teachings of the Quran & the Hadith, and the insights of modern psychology. Most importantly, you've learned that change is truly possible, and you have the power to transform your relationships, starting with the relationship you have with yourself.

Think back to the struggles you were facing when we first began this exploration together. The longing for deeper connections and a sense of belonging: these challenges are not unique to you; they are part of the human experience. Now, you are equipped with a powerful toolkit to navigate these challenges. You can choose to respond rather than react, to communicate with empathy rather than judgment, and to set boundaries that honor your needs and the needs of others.

The journey doesn't end here; it deepens. The path ahead will undoubtedly have its twists and turns. Life, as we know, is not without its challenges. Now is the time to put this knowledge into action, to weave these insights into the fabric of your daily life. Start small, practice using "I" statements in your conversations, and make a conscious effort to listen with empathy to those around you. Begin setting boundaries where needed, even if it feels uncomfortable at first. Challenge yourself to approach conflict as an opportunity for growth, using the tools of Nonviolent Communication to guide you. Take steps to find and nurture your tribe, building that circle of belonging that we all so deeply crave.

What step will you take today to polish your inner mirror? Perhaps it's having that difficult conversation you've been avoiding. Maybe it's journaling about your attachment patterns or reaching out to an old friend. Whatever it is, take that step with courage and intention. And as you continue on this path, muse on Rumi's words: "Love is the astrolabe of God's mysteries." Let love be your guiding star, illuminating your way toward deeper connection and a more meaningful life. The relationships you long for, the life you envision, are within your reach. You have the power to transform your relationships, and in doing so, your world. I believe in you, and I am honored to have shared this stage of your transformation. May your life be filled with love, kindness, and the sheer joy of belonging.

Knowest thou why thy mirror reflects not?

Because the rust has not been scoured from its face.

If it were purified from all rust and defilement,

It would reflect the shining of the Sun of God.

- Rumi

About the Author

Hello, my name is Ahmed Mustafa, and like many of you, I'm just a regular person trying to navigate this complex world we live in. I've never considered myself a scholar or an expert, but rather a curious explorer on a journey to understand life a little better.

We live in a time that's incredibly fast-paced and competitive. Everywhere we look, we're encouraged to strive for individual success, to climb the ladder, and to achieve more. It's easy to get caught up in this race, focusing on what we can achieve for ourselves. But during all this striving, I started to notice a disconnect. I realized that despite all the advancements and opportunities around us, many of us still feel a sense of unease, a feeling that something is missing.

What I've come to understand is that despite the competitive landscape of modern society, our core human desires remain the same. We all long for **connection**; to feel loved, understood, and part of something bigger than ourselves. We crave **purpose**; a sense that our lives have meaning and that we're contributing to the world in some way. We seek **security**;

not just financial stability, but also emotional and mental well-being, a feeling of safety and peace within ourselves. And we're constantly searching for a **balance**; a way to pursue our individual dreams while also fulfilling our responsibilities to our families, communities, and the world around us.

These desires, these deep-seated longings, highlight the ongoing struggle many of us face. We live in a world that often prioritizes individual success over communal well-being, and finding our place in it can feel like trying to solve a complicated puzzle. How can we be successful and also be fulfilled? How can we take care of ourselves and also take care of others?

My journey led me to the **wisdom of the East**, particularly the teachings of Rumi and the principles found within Islam. These ancient teachings, though born in a different time and place, resonated deeply with the questions I was asking about modern life. I discovered that they offered thoughtful insights into the human condition, providing guidance on how to find inner peace, heal from past hurts, and build meaningful relationships; the very things that many of us are searching for today.

I'm not here to tell you that I have all the answers. But what I can share is my own exploration of these eternal principles and how they've helped me to better understand myself and the world around me. The books I've written are a reflection of this journey. They are an attempt to bridge the gap between ancient wisdom and modern challenges, to show how the teachings of the East can offer practical solutions to the problems we face in our everyday lives.

My hope is that through these books, you'll find tools and insights that echo with your own experiences, that you'll discover a path towards greater peace, purpose, and connection, and eventually, together, we can create a world that values not just individual success, but also the well-being of us all. Because at the end of the day, we're all in this together, searching for a way to live a life that is both meaningful and fulfilling.

· · •◡·· • ··◡•··

Explore Other Rumi-Inspired Books

ISBN: 978-1-998843-46-6

ISBN: 978-1-998843-49-7